VERMONT SAMPLER

WALTER HARD

VERMONT BOOKS

MIDDLEBURY, VERMONT

BOOKS BY WALTER HARD

SOME VERMONTERS
1928. Gorham Press *(Out of print)*

SALT OF VERMONT
1931. Stephen Daye Press *(Out of print)*

MOUNTAIN TOWNSHIP
1933. Harcourt, Brace and Company *(Out of print)*
1946, 1962—Enlarged editions, Stephen Daye Press

VERMONT VINTAGE
1937. Stephen Daye Press *(Out of print)*

VERMONT VALLEY
1937. Harcourt, Brace and Company *(Out of print)*
1959. Reprinted by Vermont Books

VERMONT SALT AND VINTAGE
(Combining SALT OF VERMONT and VERMONT VINTAGE)
1946. Stephen Daye Press

THE CONNECTICUT
1947. Rinehart and Company *(Rivers of America Series)*

A MATTER OF FIFTY HOUSES
1952. Vermont Books

VERMONT NEIGHBORS
1960. Vermont Books

THIS IS VERMONT
(with Margaret Hard)
1936. Stephen Daye Press *(Out of print)*

x x x x x x x x x x x x x x x x x x x
x   x
x   VERMONT SAMPLER   x
x   x
x x x x x x x x x x x x x x x x x x x

Most of these poems have appeared in the *Manchester* (Vermont) *Journal,* and in the *Rutland* (Vermont) *Herald.* To them grateful acknowledgement is made.

PRINTED IN THE UNITED STATES OF AMERICA

Walter Hard is poet, annalist, anecdote finder. I find his Yankees more fascinating than most of the Greeks in Greek mythology. He and I are of the same school in believing that an anecdote of sufficient pith and portent is in essence a true poem. I treasure and reread his volumes.

—CARL SANDBURG

Timepiece

Waiting for the crowd to gather,
The auctioneer was putting a table before the front door.
An old man leaned against a tree and watched.
He said the Doctor had died ten years before.
They'd just got around to settle the estate.
"How old? He'd 'a been eighty-two if he'd lived to now.
That ain't old; I'm eighty-seven."
He tried to square his bent shoulders.
"Oldest man in the village now" he added.
The blacksmith's chimney, on a corner of the Village Green,
Poured forth a cloud of black smoke.
On the other side there was a red brick church
And back of it the weather-beaten stones of the burying ground.
There the Doctor rested undisturbed by midnight calls.
"Take out those telephone poles and those automobiles,
It'd look just as it did the day the Doctor set up here.
I started drivin' for him a few months later."
He stopped to listen to the auctioneer for a minute.
"Drove 'til he died; had t' keep horses
For winter and mud time even after he got him a car."
The auctioneer was getting bids on the Doctor's big chair
And his desk, strangely free of bottles and papers.
After a while a clock was put out on the table.
It had gilded pillars on the corners
And wood sides made to look like marble.
At once the old man was alert.
He bid a quarter.
He followed the rising bids, a quarter at a time,
Until they got up to two thirty.
The old mans voice was shaking when he made it forty.
He tried to look unconcerned when the auctioneer asked for more.
"First and last time. Are you all done?"
The old man begged with his eyes as he looked around.
"Who'll make it fifty? Forty I'm offered.
All done?"
It seemed minutes to the old man before he said:
"Sold to that man over by that tree."
The old man pushed through the crowd.

He came back and set the clock on the marble carriage block.
He opened the back and let the hammer fall.
"I've set and heered that strike many a night
Waitin' fer the Doctor t' get his things ready,
Whilst the wind was slappin' th' snow against th' winder."
He shut the back and ran his hand over the smooth top.
"Yes, this old clock ticked the Doctor out
And now I reckon mebbe it'll tick me out too."
He put it under his arm and started across the Green,
The gong sounding as he stepped.

Needing a Change

The Grover farm lay on the top of the ridge
Which separated the two valleys.
The road to it, steep and winding,
Was always known as the "Hill Road."
Whoever had cleared the land on the hill top
Had found rich soil waiting,
Made by the trees he'd cut to clear it.
The long lines of stone walls
Which marked the boundaries
Were monuments to the unending toil
Of the men who had harvested the never-ending crop of stones.
Elijah Grover was the third generation on the place.
He'd taken over in his early twenties.
He was tall and rawboned and a glutton for work.
He never kept a hired man for long
For he expected him to do as much as he himself did.
He was standing by the iron kettle
Which was half inside the barnyard and half out.
Ice cold water from a sure spring poured into it.
Elijah was talking to a man in a car.
"Yes sir" he was saying,
"I'm seventy-eight, or I will be next month if I live."
The visitor thought he seemed rugged enough
So he should easily make his birthday at least.
"Well I've had the bitter with th' sweet.
Seventy-eight year of it's quite a spell.
Ain't been feeling too good this winter."
He put his foot on the water kettle.
"Sometimes I wonder if it agrees with me here" he added.

Guide For Guests

Amos lived alone near the top of the mountain.
He did a little trapping
And each year's town report showed
He'd received wages for work on the road.
Of course he had a good garden and a woodlot
And take it all in all he managed very well.
The fall after the big flood
He worked more than usual on the road.
Then he worked down the valley on a WPA job
But the long cold ride in the pickup truck they sent
Was too uncomfortable and he quit.
He was sitting by the kitchen table.
The teakettle was singing on the stove
While outside the snow was falling in big flakes.
On the table Amos had a bottle of ink and some paper.
He was composing a letter.
His labor-knotted hands were not used to holding
Such a delicate tool as a pen
And his spelling vocabulary was limited.
When a neighbor dropped in he was glad of an excuse
To rest from his epistolary labors.
He felt he must explain the unusual task
He had been caught at.
"I got me money saved up t' go vis'tin' " he said.
"Callate t' go to my cousin's to Boston.
Got me enough saved up t' get me there and some fer presents.
Writin' her I'm acomin'."
"If you only got enough t' git there
How 'are you figurin' t' git back home?"
Amos reached for a stick of wood.
"That's their hunt" he said.

Contrast at the County Seat

The road drops quickly to the village.
There the Green spreads out on either side.
On the left stands the County House
Offering hospitality to the traveler,
While on the end of the hostelry
Are the barred windows of the county jail.

The County House is old and sedate in spite of the row
Of gayly painted chairs on its long porch.
There is the store still showing the simple lines
Of its ancient architecture in spite of the shining windows
Which reflect the row of red gas pumps
Where the hitching posts used to stand.
On the right the rambling tavern
Remains true to its pristine dignity,
Spotless in its white paint.
Beyond there is the house built for worship.
Between it and the tavern stands the court house,
Whose tall fluted pillars cast shadows on its white front—
A classic monument to the ancient dignity of the Law.
On the hills, plows are turning long straight furrows
And harrows are making fields smooth for planting.
Along the street women bend over flower beds
Behind white picket fences.
Joyful children race around the school yard,
Free for a moment from life's drudgeries.
The south wind stirs the new green leaves on the maples.

     · · · · · · · · ·

Inside the classic court house
A man is on trial for his life,
Accused of murdering a Chinaman.

No Margin for Error

When Young Jim began to work in the bank
Some of the older men in the village
Were not quite sure he was fitted for the job.
Of course his father was still there all the time
But he was getting along in years.
Not that they had anything against Young Jim
But he hadn't steadied down.
He liked to go out to dances
And some said he played cards considerable too.
Then he played in the band.
That didn't seem quite suited to the dignity
They expected to find in their banker.
They couldn't do much about it
Because Old Jim practically owned the bank.

Gradually Young Jim made himself solid
With most of the uncertain elders
By his pleasant manner and willingness to listen.
So it came about that often Old Jim
Wouldn't go to the bank for several days
Leaving his son to run things alone.
One morning just after Young Jim had pulled up the shades
Eber Stevens came in and asked for some change.
He put down a twenty dollar bill.
"Goin' out t' peddle a beef I jest killed.
Don't figger on havin' t' trust nobody
'Cause I can't make change either."
Jim counted out the silver in piles
And shoved them under the grating.
"Guess that'll fix you up" he said,
As he went back to his book work.
After some time he looked up and saw Eber
Still standing there counting and restacking.
He put his pen back of his ear and got down from the stool.
"Didn't I give you enough?" he asked.
Eber's lips went on counting the last pile.
He stopped and looked at the money.
"I say, didn't I give you enough?" Jim repeated.
Eber sighed. "Jest barely" he said.

Alone

She was sitting on the kitchen porch.
From the south meadow the breeze
Brought the familiar summer sound of the mowing machine.
There wasn't any need to hurry with the peas she was shelling.
He wasn't riding that mowing machine.
He wouldn't be coming up to the watering trough with the team.
He wouldn't be washing his hot face with the cold water at the sink.
It had all happened so quickly
And her even-going mind caught up with changes slowly.
He'd never been sick before.
Any idea that his strong body might break
Had never come to make her ready for tragedy.
Others had come in to take charge.
As she looked back she felt as though
She had only come to the surface now and then.

Gradually she was piecing the whole thing together;
Filling in the gaps to make the days whole.
After the funeral there had been the family matters
Most of which had been settled by his relations.
Almost before she knew it there had been the auction
And the crowds of buyers and cruious ones.
She saw the herd he'd nurtured sold off in two hours.
She saw strangers dragging his hard-won farm machines away.
And now a neighbor was cutting the hay in the south meadow.
She was sitting alone on the kitchen porch
With no one to wait for.
The neighbors had been very kind
But she wasn't used to sharing with anyone but him—
Joy or sorrow.
She appreciated what people tried to say
But she couldn't think of anything to say back.
That very morning the young minister had been up.
He'd brought some flowers from his wife.
"You miss your husband very much" he had said.
"Yes" she said, rocking slowly,
"I've washed his shirts for over forty years."

Independence

Pete Goodman was never able to keep a job
More than a few months at most.
Usually it was a matter of weeks.
The odd thing was that his employers
Were usually sorry to lose him.
He was a good workman and handy at anything,
But he could stand just so much bossing.
Then even mildly delivered requests
Stirred him to rebellion as much as downright orders.
He'd quit on the spot or not show up next day.
Rarely did arguments have any effect.
They usually brought forth more caustic rejoinders.
When Pete enlisted in the army for a three year term
About the time of the Spanish war
People in the village couldn't understand it.
Pete as a soldier didn't make sense.
They fully expected he'd be shot as a deserter
Before he'd been in a month.

Instead, when his first term ended,
He reenlisted for another three years.
When he was home on furlough once
One of his former short-term employers
Met him on the street.
He finally asked him how he stood army discipline.
"Did you ever throw down your gun and stamp your foot
And tell 'em to go to hell, when they gave an order?"
Peter looked at the speaker and then at the ground.
With the trace of a grin, almost in a whisper, he said:
"Once."

Time for Sleep

To all of the family, even to second cousins,
He was always known as "Uncle Ned."
The neighbors' children, who grew up playing around the house,
Called him "Uncle Ned" too.
He was the kind of man everybody would like
To claim as a relative.
He had never had any children of his own.
His only son had died with his mother at birth.
Perhaps because he hadn't any of his very own
To give his affection to
He had enough to spread around in a bigger circle.
In the summer the farmhouse was always full of visiting family.
As the years went by there were more and more
So that often there were three generations around the table.
Even when Uncle Ned was over eighty
He always looked forward to having the house full.
He'd often doze off in the midst of things
But he always insisted on being there.
His manner of getting folks off to bed
Had always been a joke in the family.
He'd wind the two clocks: the grandfather's one in the hall,
And the marbelized one on the living room mantel.
Then he'd go out onto the porch
And look at the thermometer and then the sky.
No matter what the outlook he'd always come in and say:
"It's a good night to sleep."
The summer he was eighty-five he slept much in his own room.
Then one morning they knew he would never waken.
That evening his favorite nephew

Stood on the porch trying to fit death into life.
Finally he turned toward the window
Of Uncle Ned's bedroom.
"Well Uncle Ned" he said
"It's a good night to sleep."

A Hot Spell

Even Deacon Stoddard, who was reputed
To wear his red flannels all summer,
Admitted it was "pretty warm."
The shades at the windows along the street
Were drawn down before the sun came up
To bottle up the night's refreshing coolness.
In the morning there was some activity
Around the store and postoffice
But soon after noon the deserted street
Shimmered in the scorching summer sun.
Brayley had moved his chair from the store porch
To a shady spot under the maple across the street.
He'd even taken off his black alpaca coat
And, with his chair tipped back,
He slept undisturbed.
Two small boys ambled along the highway
Savoring the hot dust with their bare feet.
The screen door of Brayley's slammed
And Brayley arose rubbing his eyes.
He hurried over to get two bottles of root beer
From the icy coolness of his refrigerator.
He returned to his chair but not to his nap.
The hot breeze brought the busy whirr of a mowing machine
And then the keen ring of a stone on a scythe.
A buckboard, sagging with the weight of Hen Sawyer,
Came slowly around the corner by the store.
He stopped by the hitching bar and Brayley got up,
This time taking his chair with him.
As he approached, Hen was wiping his brow with a blue handkerchief.
"Been a hot day if a feller was hayin' " he said—
"But I wa'n't."

An Error in Energy

It was a dull time in the village.
Winter was petering out and most of the winter jobs,
Such as getting in ice and wood, had been done.
It was too early to do anything about spring work
So the congregation around Brayley's stove
Was fairly large and steady in its attendance.
Rob Emerson casually remarked one day
That he wished he could get their piano moved upstairs.
There wasn't anybody to play it since his daughter had married
And it just stood in the sitting room taking up space.
Howard Duffy asked how Rob's cider was.
Rob opined he had a goodly supply on hand.
"Well" Howard said, "you furnish cider of the proper horsepower,
And I'll get me a crew t' move it up for yu."
He got a sheet of wrapping paper and a stub of a pencil.
After covering a lot of space with figures he announced
That if the cider was as stated, figuring the usual weight
Of a normal-sized piano, it would take four glasses per man
For four men to move the instrument up one flight.
The next night Howard and his three helpers were at Rob's door.
Having taken aboard the four glasses of cider each
As well as several of Mrs. Emerson's doughnuts,
They moved into the sitting room where the piano stood.
Mrs. Emerson closed the kitchen door
And went to work washing the glasses
And orderizing the kitchen.
She heard the heavy tread of the men as they moved into the hall.
With Howard shouting orders
And the others doing considerable grunting,
They moved onward and upward.
After what seemed a long time to Mrs. Emerson
They came down and went out the front door.
Rob came in and sat down by the kitchen table.
"What's th' matter?" she said, "Did yu strain yourself?"
"Nope. I didn't do no liftin' t' speak of."
"Well, what you so glum about. Piano's moved ain't it?"
Rob sighed. "We didn't figger suthin' right.
We was wrong on what a feller could do on four glasses o' cider."
Mrs. Emerson stood in front of her husband.
"What on earth you talkin' about. It's upstairs ain't it?"
Rob straightened up and fairly shouted:
"Upstairs? Hell, it's in the attic."

Something Missing

Standing in the road where the bus had dropped him
Ira gazed up the hill where a winding road climbed.
He could hardly believe he'd landed at the right spot.
He remembered a few trees along the wall that held the road
But now, except where it looped into the meadow,
The whole road was hidden by trees.
All he could see of the farmhouse was one end of the roof
And the kitchen chimney from which smoke was drifting.
As he went up the road he noticed
That it wasn't half as steep as he'd remembered it.
And that rock out in the meadow—
Well of course it might have weathered away with the years.
They'd always called it "Big Rock."
The apple orchard too had shrunk
Even though the trees were years older.
He hoped the present owner would have a few of those apples
So he could show the fellows in the office
Why he was always talking about the fruit his father raised.
A week later Ira was back at his office desk.
In spite of some outdoor color on his cheeks
He looked older and he was much quieter.
For years he'd been telling the various young folks
Who moved in and out of the office
About the terribly steep hill he used to slide on
In front of the farmhouse.
They all knew about the enormous rock near the turn
And especially they knew of the wonderful big apples.
When he'd come back from his visit
They'd gathered around his desk to hear how things looked
After forty-odd years absence.
One asked about the hill and another about the big rock.
And others remembered those wonderful apple trees.
Some of the older ones realized
That a change had come over Ira.
He seemed to have lost something.
At first he spoke with some of his old enthusiasm,
But it only lasted a few minutes.
"Yes" he said finally, with a faraway look in his eyes,
"The hill was there, and the rock was there,
And the apple trees—they were all there."

He stopped and fingered something on his desk:
Then he added, almost in a whisper:
"But the boy wasn't."

For Whom Did The Bell Toll?

For over a century the red brick church
Had stood a stalwart sentinel on the hill.
It's supporters had grown fewer and fewer
Until it was closed much of the time,
Since there was no longer a settled minister.
Then a group of summer residents began to take an interest.
Arrangements were made for a summer supply
And a meeting was called of all those interested
To make arrangements for the opening service.
One of the older members suggested that the old custom
Of ringing the bell an hour before service,
So it could send its invitation up and down the valley,
Be revived, as well as having it tolled
As the minister mounted to the pulpit.
He was deeply moved as he spoke of what that bell had meant
For many years in the life of the village.
The idea was taken up with such enthusiasm
That few noticed elderly Miss Cutler's evident dissent.
She sat on the edge of her chair shaking her head
And trying to attract the attention of the moderator.
Finally someone sitting next obtained a hearing for her.
She arose with some difficulty and her voice trembled
As she told the silent group why she couldn't stand it
If they ever tolled that old bell again.
"The last time that bell was tolled
Was on the occasion of the death of our beloved President,
Our dear Calvin Coolidge."
She faltered and then went on.
"I shall never forget that day
Of tragic loss to our country.
I just couldn't bear to hear that solemn sound again."
She turned to find her chair.
As she sat down she said in a stronger voice;
"Or mebbe it was President Harding."

A Mitigating Circumstance

Of course during the two years
The young minister had stayed in the village
He had not escaped some criticism.
Being the successor to Dr. Anderson,
Who had served the church for forty-odd years,
It was natural that some of the older members
Found a stranger in the pulpit hard to bear.
However the young minister—and he was usually called that—
Was very tactful and made his changes slowly.
Gradually the empty pews began to be filled.
By the end of his second year the church was done over
And at that time several relics of the past
Disappeared, especially some portraits
From the "Ladies Parlor" in the basement of the church.
This aroused the ire of Deacon Elmer.
He was only mollified when the young minister
Explained how unworthy of these fathers in Israel
The crayon portraits really were.
The Deacon immediately made arrangements for an oil of himself
To be made from special photographs after his demise
By adding a codicil to his will.
When it was reported that the young minister
Had received a call to a much larger church
There was a feeling of sorrow all over the village.
Only Deacon Elmer failed to express regret.
He kept a tight-mouthed silence
And people generally thought it was the picture episode
Which still rankled in his bosom.
Finally Ned Stiles said to the Deacon
That he just couldn't understand his attitude.
"Some say you're even glad he's going" Ned said.
The Deacon was silent for a minute, then he said:
"No, that ain't it at all.
I'm sorry he's goin' but they's another side to it.
He's brought our church suthin' of an honor
It ain't never had before."
He shut his mouth tight and looked at Ned.
"Did you ever stop t' think that he's th' first minister
Our church ever had, t' my knowledge,
That anybody else wanted?"

A Tale of a Pig

Mrs. Anita Belmont had lived in her new home
Only one summer.
She had bought the Aiken place one fall
And had it made over during the winter.
She had left the old barn with its sag
Because it was picturesque, only adding a coat of red paint.
When she had come up in the spring
A problem at once presented itself.
She found that the young man who had collected her garbage
Had been drafted and had gone off to war.
She finally consulted the Farm Bureau agent in the village
About her need for a garbage remover.
"Well, Miss Belmont, as I recall it
You still have the old hog pen back of the barn, haven't you?"
She reported it still stood there
But that it had been thoroughly cleaned and painted.
"Well why not buy a little pig, Miss Belmont?
Feed what 's edible, for a hog, to it,
Add a little grain perhaps,
And in the autumn you'll have quite a respectable hog.
Be helping with the food supply too."
Following his advice a small pig was duly installed in the pen.
There was considerable company at Miss Belmont's
And the cook liked the guest back of the barn
So the supply of pork grew daily.
Late that fall Miss Belmont again called the Farm Agent.
She was going back to the city and what should she do
With the good-sized pig in her pen.
The Agent told her he knew of a nearby farmer
Who might be interested and that he would call him up.
In due time the farmer presented himself at Miss Belmont's.
He looked the pig over.
"Good lookin' hog" he said,
"How much you cal'latin' he ought t' fetch?"
Miss Belmont said: "Well, my goodness,
I hate to part with the little creature at any price.
However, I must.
Let me see now. I paid ten dollars for him
When he was a baby. Let me see—
Of course we've had the use of him all summer.
Would you think five dollars would be too much now?"

In Wartime

The mellow wind bent the grass making a light green wave
That billowed along the hill toward the brook.
Under an elm, black and white cows stood.
Birds flew here and there.
Their songs made ripples in the flowing rustle of the leaves.
Across the valley there was a farmhouse,
And a gray barn and a leaning silo.
Bush-covered stone walls hid the road
That climbed the hill slantwise to get a better footing.
There was a row of maples near the farmhouse—
Fulfilled promises made to some thoughtful forebear,
Long since done with promises and planting.
Meadows, pastures, plowed land with brush division lines;
And cloud shadows drifting over all the precise patterns,
Paying no heed to fences or earth's ideas of order.
Up the slope the gray shadows crept
To fade against the green wall of mountain.
All the sounds were gentle,
Each fitting in to make silence into sound
Without robbing silence.
The smooth pastures curved to the green hills
Which took them to the mothering serenity of the mountain.
Peace lured the soul.
How to be a part of this tranquil pattern,
How to hold forever this elemental peace,
And still not be a tree or grass or four-footed beast!

Rest for the Weary

It had been a tough winter for everybody.
Snow had fallen in early December
And kept piling up week after week.
Even the usual January thaw had made little impression
Though it had made the going about impossible.
Dr. Mosely had been run ragged.
He generally kept a single horse
As a sort of spare when his team was overworked.
Jim Vetal was his driver and general assistant.
This winter he had to hire a team from the livery stable
Several times to give the Doctor's horses a rest.

But there was no rest for the Doctor.
One night in late February Jim was letting the team walk
As they came into the village street.
The worn Doctor was asleep on the seat beside him.
He suddenly came to and told Jim
To let him out at the Holland's house.
He would walk the little way from there.
Mrs. Holland had been very sick for some weeks.
She'd seemed better that morning when he stopped
But he'd sleep better if he stopped in just for a minute.
Mrs. Holland was a large woman and very well upholstered.
As the Doctor came into the room he noticed
That her breathing certainly was much better.
He felt her pulse, holding his worn silver watch.
Then he said he'd just listen to her heart a minute.
There were no such things in those days
As stethoscopes or any mechanical hearing aids.
The physician got his knowledge first hand.
So he pressed his ear over Mrs. Holland's heart.
He told her to start counting slowly
And not to stop until he told her.
She started—"one—two—three—four—five————"
The tired Doctor found himself in a comfortable position
Sitting in a low chair with his head on a soft warm pillow.
He heard "twenty-six—twenty-seven————"
Then off in the distance he heard a voice:
"Five thousand seven hundred and fifty-two,
Five thousand seven hundred and fif————"
The Hollands could never say enough
In praise of Dr. Mosely.
Worn out as he had been he had sat up half the night
To make sure of the safety of his patient.

She Hung On Her Words

In spite of the fact that most people
Felt the loss of him to be an addition to the place,
When Hen Dilt was found—
A piece of permanently suspended animation
In the attic of the old Dilt house—
Not a hint of anything but real sympathy
Came to the long-suffering sister with whom he had lived.

Never in the long years of making excuses for Hen
Did Lettie ever drop one word of criticism.
He had been left to her care by an overindulgent mother
Who had spoiled him from the day he was born.
Probably many of the neighbors
Felt that this final act was the most worthwhile thing
Hen had ever undertaken.
All of the neighbors had been in to see Lettie
And many had been interested in a glimpse at Hen.
Curious crowds had stood around looking at the house,
And the attendance at the funeral
Would have honored the most influential citizen.
Luella Pease had not been over to visit with Lettie
Although she had left some baked beans at the back door.
After the excitement had somewhat died down
Luella told her mother she was going over to see Lettie.
Her mother, knowing her happy faculty
For putting her foot in it,
Warned her to be careful about what she said,
And by no means to mention anything that would in any way
Bring Hen's manner of taking-off to mind.
Luella seemed shocked that her mother should mention such a thing.
Arriving at the house Luella started with the weather.
She said she was always glad to have it pleasant on Monday.
"I always say to Ma I'm glad if it's pleasant on Monday
On account of if it rains all the washings that don't dry."
Lettie agreed and remarked that Luella and her mother
Had a nice porch to use in case it rained.
"Yes" Luella said, "that's a fact, and your porch is too narrow."
Thinking that might seem critical, she hastened to add:
"But of course you've got a nice attic
To hang things in."

Christmas 1945

It was all just as he remembered it:
The long village street with the irregular Green
About half-way down.
There were wreaths in windows and on doors,
And colored lights that would come to life at night.
Yes, and there was the big tree on the edge of the Green.
He was glad they had all these things back,

Just as they used to be before he had gone away.
He thought, as he drove along slowly,
Of all the strange places where he'd remembered that street.
The thought of it had often been the thing
That kept him going ahead—
Remembering to make himself forget.
He found so many packages
In the post office at Brayley's store,
That he had to make two trips to the pickup truck.
When he came back for the second lot
Old man Peters, who was sitting back of the stove,
Stuck his head out and said:
"Well Charlie, looks as though you'd bought out
A hul city store on your way back from discharge camp."
Charlie, who had almost forgotten the life of four years back,
Suddenly felt the home warmth in the old man's bantering tone.
After he had gone out, old man Peters shook his head.
"Can't see how they stood what they did.
I recollect, musta been 'bout a year ago now,
Charlie's father had a letter tellin' as how
The boy's outfit had got caught there in It'ly,
Been under shell fire fer a week, day and night.
Course Charlie spoke of dodgin' high explosives,
Makin' light of it.
I recollect he spoke of spendin' th' night
In a barn with the front blowed away."
Brayley sat with a far away look in his eyes.
Then he said:
"I recollect that letter.
I know it come just this time o' year.
The boy said he slep' in a manger."

Aunt Betsy

That small unpainted house almost hidden by bushes
Had been Aunt Betsy's home since childhood.
In the early days the yard had been kept up
But when all the work about the place
Had to be done by Aunt Betsy herself,
The front yard gradually went its own way.
Aunt Betsy never used the front door
And everybody got used to following the path to the back.

There they'd find her on pleasant days
Busy in her garden or with her chickens.
She'd invite them to sit down on her back porch
And she'd bring out some of her homemade wine—
Elderberry, currant or dandelion.
She was never too busy to stop for a visit.
She didn't mind a little gossip now and then
But she never let her love of spice
Over-flavor anything she passed around.
During the best of the year she went to the village,
Usually getting a lift from someone passing.
She always carried a basket on her arm.
She might have eggs in it for the store
Or she might have a mess of peas to leave at someone's door.
Often she carried a bunch of flowers for someone who was sick.
Many people said a call from Aunt Betsy when you were sick
Was as good as a dose of tonic.
One day she was on her way home from the village
When a car stopped and a man asked her to ride.
She'd never seen him or the woman beside him
But she never hesitated when a ride was offered.
She leaned forward sitting on the edge of the back seat.
As usual she set out to find who these people were.
They seemed to know who she was and where she lived.
Then it came to her who they might be.
"You ain't the new principal up to the Academy by any chance?"
The car was slowing up in front of her house.
"Yes, that's right" he said, "and this is my wife."
As the car stopped Aunt Betsy shook hands with them.
"Thanks very much for the ride and meetin' you—well—
"I've been havin' a better time than I thought I was."

O Sweet Content

The Professor and his wife had stayed
Much later than they ever had since they bought the place.
For the first time there were no waiting classes
For the Professor to get back to.
The long awaited retirement
Which he'd looked forward to and dreaded had come.
The week before the opening of the University
He had found himself in the hurried state of mind

That those days had brought on for nearly a half-century.
Then he gradually realized he didn't have to go to anything.
Today life still seemed good to him as he turned from the fire
To his favorite view down the valley.
The cold gray clouds portended snow
And the warmth of the fire was cheering.
He almost wished they hadn't planned to go South,
Even though that had long been a cherished part
Of the retirement years' plan.
He tried to imagine how it would look
When snow covered the valley.
He recalled his boyhood days on hills not so far away.
John Burke came in with an armful of wood,
Maple, fresh cut and smelling of sap.
The Professor spoke of that smell
Which reminded him of maple sugar time.
"Do you find yourself sort of dreading the winter, John?"
John leaned over the hearth and shook the snow and sawdust
From his sheep-lined coat.
"Wal, Perfessor, it's this way with me."
He took off his cap and leaned against the mantel.
"Come late November, settin' by th' kitchin stove,
I sez t' myself, I sez:
"M' shed's full o' wood and th' barn's full o' hay;
We got a barr'l o' flour in th' butt'ry
And a crock er more o' pork and some fair cider down cellar.
And settin' there b' the kitchin stove
I hitches up m' heavy wool socks
And I sez t' m' self, I sez,
'LET 'ER SNOW b' Judast, LET 'ER SNOW!'."

A Generous Target

Lawyer Sears was a born gambler.
Taking a chance was his chief delight.
When he began his practice he was always taking chances,
Usually long ones, on many of his clients.
As his practice increased he grew more conservative
As far as his professional services went.
Otherwise he was forever buying real estate
Or almost anything where there was a gamble involved.
His poker game was that of an expert

And he rarely missed a week without at least one evening
Devoted to serious poker playing.
Mrs. Sears was much opposed to any card playing
And when, after they had been married a short time,
She found that her husband not only played cards,
Which she had known, but that he played for money
She was so upset that he gave up cards entirely for some years.
Gradually he got back into his old habits
When he was attending court in other places
And in due time his wife accepted his sinning
Though in no way condoning it.
All of Lawyer Sears' churchgoing religion
Was in his wife's name,
And she was faithful enough to cover two souls' salvation.
She often brought visiting clergymen home to meals
Hoping, perhaps, to stir some churchly interest in her husband.
One Sunday, a supply minister during the regular one's vacation
Had, in the course of his sermon,
Made some scorching remarks about the growing habit of gambling.
Knowing he was to dine at the Sears', one of the congregation,
A former friend of the clergyman,
Warned him of Lawyer Sears' gambling propensities.
The young minister, deciding to clear the air at once,
As soon as he had said grace turned to Lawyer Sears,
"Mr. Sears, while retracting nothing of what I said,
I trust if you hear of some remarks I made this morning
You will not feel that there was anything personal meant.
You see I, er————"
Lawyer Sears held the carving knife and fork
Poised over the Sunday roast.
"Don't worry a mite, young man" he said.
"It would be an uncommonly weak sermon
That didn't hit me somewhere."

The Latest Decision

The usual after-dinner struggle to keep awake
Was obviously going on in the court room.
One of the side judges was shielding his closed eyes
By resting his head on his spread out hand.
The presiding judge leaned forward in his chair,
Either straining to hear, or to keep awake, or both.

From the open window came the sawing of a locust
And now and then the clatter of a passing wagon.
The officers of the court, the sheriff and constables,
Had tipped their chairs back against the wall
And were sleeping peacefully.
Most of the jurors were paying attention to the witness
Except for one old man in the back row
Who kept drifting off and then coming to with a start.
Then he'd look around to see if anyone noticed.
The defending lawyer was a nattily dressed New Yorker.
There was nothing sleepy about him
As he fired questions at the rather slow-witted witness.
The local prosecuting attorney sat slouched in his chair
With his long legs stretched out in front of him.
The visiting attorney snapped out a question.
Very deliberately the local lawyer said;
"I object to that question, Your Honor."
The Judge looked through his bushy eyebrows and barked:
"Objection sustained."
The New York attorney faced the court.
In a rather patronizing tone he informed the court
That a very recent decision had been handed down
Which would make the evidence in question admissible.
Looking around at the jury and audience he added, smiling,
"Probably news of this most recent decision
Has not as yet penetrated to these remote parts."
The Judge leaned over toward the attorney.
"This court just handed down a decision to the effect
That this evidence is not admissible.
If the learned gentleman from New York
Knows of any more recent decision than that,
This court will be glad to hear about it."

An Isolationist

Oliver Humper's farm was on a side road
On a hill to the east of the village.
The upper meadow ended in a stone wall
Which separated it from a rocky pasture.
This was gradually ended by the ever-encroaching woods.
Oliver and his wife were the only remnants
Of a family which had once filled the farmhouse.

They had finally taken care of the old folks
And then been left there, childless, to keep the place going.
After his parents died Oliver bought some acres
Up on the mountain adjoining his own land.
He bought it cheap and folks thought he was wise.
Next he bought some land on the other side
That adjoined his pasture to the south.
Then he bought a rock-ribbed piece, north,
With nothing much on it but scrub pine.
There would never be any good timber on it,
Not in Oliver's time at any rate.
Then the opinion makers around the store stove
Began to wonder what had come over Oliver.
He'd kept right on buying, first on one side and then on another.
One day when they heard his back line had moved again
By the acquisition of more mountain land,
Oliver dropped into the store.
Old man Stevens decided he'd find out
Whether Oliver was plain crazy, as he suspected, or not.
So he asked Oliver what he thought he was doing
Buying up all of outdoors this way.
Oliver looked over his glasses and said:
"Don't like t' have folks ownin' land next t' mine.
That's why."

Population Center

On a hill the white tapering spire
Rose above the green leaves of the maples.
The faded red brick church with its white pillars
Was almost hidden by the big trees.
Two grass-grown tracks curved up from the road.
They led to the worn marble steps.
The sun shining through the leaves
Made shifting shadows on the fluted columns.
The columns made still, slanting shadows on the flagstones.
The grass-grown tracks led back of the church
To a stone wall covered with vines.
There was an iron gate
And beyond rows of stones, gray and moss-spotted,
And glistening monuments set in hedged plots.
An old man in checked gingham overalls and jumper
Was straightening one of the moss-spotted stones

30

Which stood near the gate.
A stranger came into the burying ground.
He had his coat under his arm and his straw hat in his hand.
"Say, are you acquainted around here?" he asked the old man.
"Lived here all m' life—so fur"
The old man said, straightening up a joint at a time.
The stranger didn't smile.
"Well I've been walking dusty roads in this burg
'Til I'm about worn out.
What I want to find is the thickly-settled part, if there is any."
The old man made a sweeping gesture toward the graveyard.
"Well sir" he said, "You're right plumb in the midst of it
Here and now."

Too Much To Expect

Rollin had been trying to get to his woodlot
Ever since there had been enough snow for sledding.
At last the day had come when the winter road was open
And the prospects for a good day were bright.
He got up long before daylight and lit the kitchen fire.
Then he went out and fed his horse and the cows.
When he came in his wife had breakfast ready—
Fried salt pork and potatoes and a steaming pot of coffee.
She had his lunch put up in a pail
And, when Rollin tucked it under the hay for the horse,
He felt of the jug of cider he'd smuggled in.
By the time the sun came over the mountain
Rollin was well up on the road.
He had on his worn buffalo coat
With an old surcingle around it for a belt.
He had a red handkerchief tied outside of the turned-up collar.
His frosty breath made icicles on his whiskers.
About nine Rollin turned off the broken road.
A smooth white stretch, a little wider than the sled,
With trees on either side showed the way to the woodlot.
He soon emerged into the clearing where he'd cut the year before.
He took off the mare's bridle and tied her halter to a tree.
He gave her the hay and picked up the cider jug.
He had to tip it quite a bit more
Than he did when he'd started up the mountain.
He ate a little of his lunch and then hung his coat on a bush.

31

He was ready for the day's chopping.
Later, when he came into the kitchen,
His wife looked up from putting something into the oven.
"Well good lands!" she said, looking at the clock,
"What on earth fetched you back now?
You couldn't 'a more 'n got up there and come back,
Let alone doin' any choppin'."
Rollin sat down in the corner and pulled his moccasin rubbers off.
"Had a mite o' hard luck" he mumbled.
"Matter of fact I forgot m' axe."
His wife was stunned to silence for only a minute.
Finally she ran out of words and breath and turned away.
Rollin hung his mittens on a line over the stove.
"Gosh a' mighty" he said, "y' can't expect a feller
T' remember everythin'."

Let 'em Set

While there were still signs of winter
Around clumps of bushes or on the north slopes
There was spring in the air.
The crows proclaimed it from the meadows.
Cattle, long winter-bound, cavorted with high-kicking awkwardness.
Kitchen doors along the road stood open
And the yards showed the collected rubbish of winter.
School children carried unwanted coats on their arms
As they raced toward the school yard.
A sailor was walking along the road toward the pass,
Through which the road crossed the mountains.
He carried a duffle bag on his shoulder.
His cap was shoved back on his head
And he whistled as he drank in the tonic of spring.
As a noisy pickup approached the sailor turned
And waited for it to come abreast.
A lank bearded figure opened the door with a broken glass.
He was still clad for below-zero weather
And his cap was pulled down over his ears.
The sailor threw his bag into the back and climbed in.
"Some day" he said with enthusiasm.
The driver nodded as he dropped in the chattering clutch.
Several times the sailor tried to make conversation

But the most he got was a reluctant nod or a grunt.
As the steaming car struggled over the summit and started down
The sun was shining on the tops of the peaks to the south.
The sailor leaned forward.
"What's the name of that peak?" he asked forgetting himself.
Looking straight ahead the driver said: "Dunno."
Twisting around in the seat the sailor tried again.
"What do they call this range we've just crossed?"
He got the same reply as before, spoken a bit more distinctly.
Evidently deciding this interrogation must be stopped
The driver, after a pause, said:
"We don't pay no attention t' them things.
We jest let 'em set there."

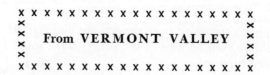

The Mountain Farm

The farm lay along the slope of the mountain
Which rose gently from the upper meadows.
What Sam Parker got from it
He wrested by main force:
Not that the land was poor,
But it was in such small pieces
With limestone ledges cropping out between.
It was one of those farms
Which never should have been divorced from the forest
Which still hovered on its flanks.
And yet three generations had lived there
And Sam's children showed no signs of want.

One summer day a man drove by
And stopped, as many did, to get the view.
The valley, a green bowl miles wide.
North, south, and east, the uneven rim of mountains,
Everchanging, eternal.
The V-shaped nick to the south
Was where Stark marched his men
On the way to the Battle of Bennington.

The next day the man came again
And brought Howard Stickles,
A lawyer who made his living
By selling insurance and real estate—
Mostly timberland until the city folks
Began to buy up abandoned farms.
After some general talk
He asked Sam if he'd ever thought of selling:
His client, here, sort of took a fancy to the view.

The upshot of it was the man made an offer
Of fifteen thousand dollars for the farm.
Stunned by just the name of so much money,
Sam asked for time to talk it over with his wife.
That night when the children were asleep upstairs,
Sam and his wife talked and planned.
They remembered all the things they'd gone without,
The hard days and wakeful nights.
These they weighed against the joys,
The real rewards of honest toil,
And the memories haunting every corner of the old
    house.
But then the freedom fifteen thousand dollars meant:
A better farm near town, and money in the bank.
Almost decided to sell, Sam lit his lantern
And went out for his nightly inspection of the barns.
Coming back he stopped on the porch.
A full moon was brooding over the sleeping valley.
He could see the mountain peaks
Gray and calm in the silvery summer night.

Here and there a light twinkled—
His neighbors though miles apart.
He called his wife.
They stood together
Awestruck at the mystery which is night among the
    mountains.
A horse pounded in his stall.
A calf bleated and its mother answered.
A dog barked,
And then the silence of the moonlit valley

The next morning coming from the creamery,
Sam saw Stickles and the man.
"The woman and I've decided.
We don't want to let the old place go.
What'd I do with fifteen thousand dollars anyhow?
It'd just be a worriment."

Smuggler's Notch

The sign over the wide door read:
AUTO REPAIRING—GAS—OIL.
As the car slowed up by the gas pump,
The garageman hurried to the door and called,
"I'll be there'n a minute. Phone's a-ringin'."
The man in the car unfolded a map
And put it on the steering wheel.
He was showing his wife the route
When the garageman came out.
He put in the gas and came to the driver's seat.
The woman asked what mountain they had just come
    over,
And about the road going north to Canada.
"Ever been up through th' notch?" the garageman asked.
They hadn't. They asked if it was on their route.
He got on the running board and pointed on the map.
"Jest turn off below th' village here t' th' left
And cross the covered bridge. That'll take yu
Right up through Smuggler's Notch and back onto your
    rud."
They asked him if it was worth the extra miles.
He seemed shocked that anyone should ask such a ques-
    tion.
He went on to tell them the legend about the smugglers,
And about the mammoth spring and waterfall.
He spoke of the wildness of the country
And about the enormous boulders
On either side of the road.
He stopped and looked up the road.
"Yes," he spoke with reverence,
"There's them boulders lyin' all 'round
Jest as the Old Gent left 'em."

Big Business

Brayley came in from the back room
With a molasses jug in his hand.
He wiped around the cork with his finger
And licked the finger with signs of relish.
As he put the jug by the front door
Where old Quimby could get it,
A youngish man came up the steps.
He greeted Brayley uncertainly
Not quite sure whether he was a customer
Or the storekeeper.
Brayley enlightened him as briefly as possible
And went to his high desk at the back.
The young man followed.
Brayley gave no signs of hearing
But the young man went on with his story.
Finally he asked the storekeeper
If he didn't have a good many bad accounts.
Brayley guessed he had a few.
"Joining our credit rating agency, Mr. Brayley,
Would prevent all such losses."
Brayley looked past the young man.
"I got a credit agent o' m' own," he said.
The young man expressed surprise and some doubt.
Brayley crossed his legs and clasped his knee.
"Wal, y' see, I bought this store from Colonel Wetherbee.
He ain't got much to do sence he sold out,
So he sets there in that chair—well—
Consid'able o' th' time."
Brayley shifted legs and went on.
"First off I was fer trustin' everybody.
Then me an' th' Colonel fixed things up.
When a feller came in that wa'n't no good
The Colonel jest tapped twice onto th' floor with his
    cane."

Brayley turned to his books.
"So, yu see, young feller,
I ain't got no sort o' use fer what you're a-sellin'."

Cabe's Jewels

Cabe lived at the Poor Farm.
When he first drifted into town, sick,
He had to live there on the town
Or else he'd have died of exposure
And been buried at the town's expense.
That spring he made the old Poor Farm
Blossom like the rose.
When his flowers won prizes at the summer flower show
People began to ask him questions.
The next year he had plenty of work
And to the amazement of the town officers
That fall he insisted upon paying for his keep.
He stayed at the Farm because he liked the company.

Cabe had a weakness for jewelry.
He wore a long chain that had been his mother's
Around his neck, and on it a dollar watch.
On the side of his cap he had a glass-studded brooch,
And he always had a pin in his ragged necktie.

One morning he was working at the summer place of Dr.
    Higgins.
The Doctor noticed the brilliance of the stone
In a new pin Cabe had in his tie.
Cabe explained that he had picked it up on the road.
The Doctor looked it over and advised Cabe to advertise.
"That's a valuable stone and the owner would pay a good
    reward,"
He said, holding it where the stone caught the light.

Three weeks later Cabe was there again and he still had
    the pin.
The Doctor spoke to him about finding the owner
Or, if he couldn't do that,
He advised him to sell it.
Cabe shook his head. "Nope, I sha'n't sell it," he said.
"Nobody came t' claim it from m' puttin' up a sign
Down to the post office neither."
"Oh, you did advertise it then?" The Doctor was re-
    lieved.
Cabe leaned his spade against his hip
And spat on his hands.
"Yep, I hed a sign up fer three weeks—
But I writ it fine
And I posted it high."

The Two Angels

When Henry Ranger had made his money,
He decided to spend it on improving himself.
He took a Cook's tour to Europe,
Being careful by habit to know the cost
Before he set sail.
He followed the itinerary to the letter.
Not once did he stay in his hotel
When the party was doing something improving.
He toured the galleries until his feet rebelled.

Among the things he brought home
Was a photograph of two marble angels.
He was especially taken with these statues
Because it had suddenly come to him
That he should do something for his home town.
He had always been on the board of managers of the
    cemetery

And he naturally thought of doing something for it.
The angels appeared on the horizon just then
And gradually a plan took shape.

The white angels, one on either gate post,
Had been in place for almost a week.
Not a soul had mentioned them to Henry.
He was puzzled and hurt.
He was looking at them with admiration,
When Jimmy Styles, the gravedigger, came out of the
    gate.
"Jimmy," Henry said, pointing to the two angels,
"How do folks in the village like those new statues?"
Jimmy glanced at the angels furtively,
"They don't mind 'em," he said, starting on.

Neighbors

Strangers often wondered about those two houses
Standing as close together as they could and not touch.
There was plenty of land in the village
And the other houses stood in the middle of the plots.
When you found out that these two neighbors
Hadn't spoken to one another for twenty-odd years,
You wondered even more that their houses almost
    touched.
Ed Bowser's house—the yellow one—stood
About in the center of the lot.
Jeremiah Lapham's lot hadn't a house on it then.
The two got into a row over the line
And Jeremiah lost the suit.
Then he went and built that house as close to the line
As he could possibly get it.
Then he rented it to a family with a lot of children.
Ed stood it for a while and then he built that addition

Just as close to Jeremiah's as he could and not trespass.
It cut all of the light off on that side of Jeremiah's house,
And it made things a little quieter for Ed
Because they never used the added rooms,
But it spoiled the looks of his place.
From time to time friends of both of them
Tried to make them give up their fight.
Neither one would make the first move.
Jeremiah died suddenly one spring
And the funeral was set for Sunday afternoon at the church.
One of the neighbors passed Ed going in the opposite direction.
"Ain't yu goin' t' th' funeral?" he asked Ed.
Ed stopped short and looked at the speaker.
"No, I'm NOT going to the funeral."
He started on and then added over his shoulder:
"I'm heartily in favor of it though."

Better Than Credit

It was back in the days
When "F.H." ran the village store.
Of course, he was a hotelman
But at various times he took over
Other lines of business for short periods.
He'd been running the store for some months
When he found his manager
Had let Henry Sawyer run up quite a bill.
"F.H." called his attention to it
And told him not to let him have anything more
Until he'd paid up.
In spite of his orders,
Somehow Henry managed to buy more on credit.
"F.H." said a few things in his decided way
And the manager agreed to put a stop to Henry.

The following Saturday "F.H." met Henry on the street.
Henry had his arms full of groceries.
"F.H." stopped him.
He looked at him with a withering glance,
Which didn't bother Henry at all.
"Henry," "F.H." said, "where'ju get those things?"
Henry shifted his packages.
"Down to your store," he said.
"Did you pay for 'em?"
Henry looked defiant.
"Nope. I had 'em booked."
"F.H." looked straight at Henry for a minute.
"Henry, I'll make a bargain with yu.
If you'll agree never to go to my store again,
I'll cross off what you've got on the books
And give you what you've got there now."
Henry hesitated. Then he said,
"Guess not, 'F.H.,'
I think I kin do better 'n that."

Seeing's Not Believing

There was a good attendance at the store.
The biting north wind made a fair excuse
To let the woodpile go for a while
And sit close to Brayley's chunk stove.
The two chairs were occupied and the bench
Made of a board set on two kegs of nails.
Even the counter was occupied except in the rare intervals
When a real customer happened to come in.
The temperature records had been gone over
With Grandpa Bull having the last say.
He always reported several degrees lower than anybody
    else
And, as he always kept records in a diary,
His reports were usually taken as final.

Job Stillson brought the news
That the Barrows boy had set up a windmill on his fence.
"By cricky, that feller's a heller, whittlin'."
Job lifted his cap to uncover his ears.
"I'll be gol darned if this ain't a double contraption
With a little mill on top of a bigger one."
Grandpa Bull opined there "wa'n't nothin' onusual 'bout
    that,"
And went on to tell about one he'd seen when he was
    young.
"But this cussed thing's different," Job insisted.
"The top one goes one way and the bottom one t'other."
Job found his audience skeptical,
And Grandpa Bull said, "It just ain't possible, that's all."
At noon Grandpa went home by way of the Barrows
    house.
The Barrows boy came along and found him
Gazing at the two mills, one going one way, the other
    another.
As Grandpa started on, the boy heard him say,
"Well, by hellum, I don't believe it!"

A Lender

The auctioneer stood by the back door
On the marble step with a slanting trough in the center
Made by three generations of heavy-shod farmers.
On the porch, chairs were piled with small things
To be offered in lots before the crowd had warmed up.
Men were bringing things out from the kitchen,
To be ready as the sale went on.
People were wandering around the house
Looking over the bigger pieces of furniture.
What had been for almost a hundred years a home
Had, since breakfast that morning,
Become a second-hand store open to all comers.

The voice of the auctioneer grew stronger
As the bidding became more active.
By noon the auctioneer had moved to the barn
Where the men had been dragging out the farm machin-
    ery.
Wagons, harnesses, plows, hay rakes, were put up.
Finally, the auctioneer turned to a rusty mowing machine.
He called for bids, making a joking remark
About the antique value of this machine.
Samuel Giddings raised it a quarter.
Sam's son edged up to his father.
"You don't want that, Pa. What yu thinkin' of!"
The bid was raised and Sam went to one-fifty.
"What in time do yu want o' that piece of junk?"
Sam's son went on. "We got a good machine now."
"Once, twice— Yu all done? Sold to Sam Giddin's."
Sam turned to his disgusted son,
"Keep yer mouth shut, will yu! I know what I'm
    doin'.
I'm gittin' this one t' lend t' the neighbors."

Help in Need

It was his last Saturday in the valley.
He had come to the village church,
Two years before, fresh from the Seminary.
As he walked along the road he remembered
How many Saturday evenings he had followed it,
Going, as he was now, to see Mrs. Camden.
He'd been called there soon after he'd come to the val-
    ley,
When her husband had been hurt in the haymow.
He'd been impressed with her quiet efficiency.
During the two years no family in the valley
Had suffered so many misfortunes.

Crops had been bad,
The barn had burned with much of the stock.
Then, only a few weeks ago, Mrs. Camden had fallen
And broken her shoulder.

The young minister stopped in front of the house.
Once again he got the view of the quiet valley,
With the mountains beyond stretching north and south,
With one high peak reaching into the sky.

He had been telling Mrs. Camden
How she had been an inspiration to him—
Her steadfast courage and quiet acceptance,
No matter what hard things came her way.
"I wonder, Mrs. Camden, if you would tell me
What verse of Scripture you have found most helpful."
Mrs. Camden shifted the bandaged shoulder.
"Well, Parson," she said after some hesitation,
"I reckon I've got the most help
Out of 'Grin and bear it.' "

South Londonderry Air

On that road that goes over the hill
Between North and South Londonderry
There used to be a thriving settlement known as MIDDLE-
TOWN.
There was a church and the schoolhouse and the "hearse
house."
That was when the town furnished the conveyance
For the citizen's last ride, usually behind the family team.
Some people remember, when they were younger,
How spooky the black hearse used to look in its house
When they climbed a slanting tree to peek through the
window.
As usual the valley with its mills along the streams

Gradually drew the people from the hills.
They even moved the church down from Middletown.
Now it's part of a garage in the village.
That large house on the left
Belonged to old Doc Collins years ago.
His two children lived there—
Emeline, an old maid, and Henry, an old bachelor.
Henry carried on the farm with the help of Nelson Clark.
Nelson wasn't always a help.
He was strong and a good worker
But his mental equipment was decidedly lacking.
One day Henry wanted to send Nelson to the village
And he told him to go and saddle the horse.
When Henry came out to tell Nelson what to do at the
    village
He found him waiting with the horse by the back door.
He started to speak and then stopped.
"Nelson," he said in his usual drawl,
"You've got that saddle on back side to."
Nelson looked at the saddle.
A crafty look came on his face as he said:
"Mebbe you don't know which way I'm goin'."

Under the Spreading Chestnut Tree

In the days when a blacksmith
Could make a good living just shoeing horses,
Ned Witten had all of the business he could handle.
He had a way with horses with a nasty temper—
He always kept one of that kind to drive himself—
And some of his customers came from other towns
Because of his reputation.
He was large in frame but he spoke softly;
Many a time he would quiet a horse shaking with fear
By talking to it and laying a reassuring hand on its flank.

As horses grew scarce Ned took on automobile work;
He got into it gradually and with some distaste.
Even when there was not enough shoeing to say so
He kept his forge and his anvil ready.

The car came to a stop by the door,
And the driver opened the window.
"Can you do some work on this car?
You do automobile work, don't you?"
Ned went to the door, his hands under his leather apron.
"Yes, sir. I can fix yer car.
I do anythin' from hoss shoein' "—
He paused—
"Down."

Each to His Last

Ezra Bump was driving along the back road
That goes over the hill to the Dent place.
It's one of those roads that seems to dread the climb.
It dallies along the brook, first one side and then the
    other.
Then, when it gets to where it can't escape the hill,
It rushes straight up without even a turn to ease the
    climb.
Ezra was letting his horse take its time,
Being in no more hurry than the road to get over the
    crest.
Around the last bend before the climb
He came on the two city men who were boarding at the
    Stiles'.
He'd passed the time of day with them the day before.
They stopped to let him pass but Ezra drew up beside
    them.
"What you fellers doin' t'day?"
Ezra turned so his feet hung over the wheel.

The men seemed surprised but admitted they had noth-
ing on hand.
"Well, now," Ezra went on, "you know, er mebbe yu
don't,
Old Man Dent died this spring. He lived over th' ridge."
Ezra nodded toward the west.
"Th' Widder's got a lot o' hay down
And nothin' in th' way o' help but a hired hand.
I'm goin' over and I thought you fellers mebbe
Might be needin' a mite o' exercise."
One of the strangers had done haying in his boyhood;
The other had never had a hay fork in his hand.
After a minute's hesitation they agreed to drive over
And give Ezra a lift with the hay.

The first load was on the rack.
Ezra wound the reins around his fork
And pulled a plug of tobacco from his pocket.
The two helpers were wiping their dripping faces.
They felt they had made a good showing
Even if the hired man, alone on his side of the load,
Had kept up with the two of them.
Ezra got his chew limbered up.
"What you fellers do fer a livin' down to th' city?"
The one who had never hayed it before leaned on his
fork;
He was feeling quite pleased with his efforts.
"Oh, I spend my time at a desk figuring insurance rates."
Ezra unwound the reins and braced his feet.
Over the side of the load, he said:
"Well, I don't s'pose I'd be any better at that
Than you be at pitchin' on hay."

After the Storm

Job Atkins was looking over his meadow.
The brook, swollen by the fall rains,
Had gone on a rampage.
Over in one corner of the meadow
It had spread a mat of silt and rocks,
Spoiling perhaps two acres of good land.
Along the roadside several old elms
Lay on the stone wall, their roots sticking up.
Judson Purdy came toward him on the road.
He had a cross-cut saw in his hand.
"Been clearin' the rud down th' hill," he said, drawing
    near.
"I never see such a tangle o' toppled trees."
Job leaned his back against the fence.
"Kinda pickin' on us, seem's though,
Flood and wind all t' once.
Noah only had th' flood.
Do any damage t' your place?"
Judson leaned on his saw.
"No, nothin' to speak of.
Water did a mite o' cuttin' back th' house.
Then th' wind blew m' hog pen clean over th' fence."
Job whistled: "Wheeuw!"
"I didn't know nothin' of it till mornin'.
I went down t' feed th' stock;
Th' hog pen wan't to be seen,
And there set that durned hog
Madder'n hell."
"Can't say as I blame 'im," Job said.

Winter Comes to Tinmouth Valley

The road wound through the winter woods
Where the shadows of trees lay on the smooth snow.
It dipped down to a small brook

With frost-covered bushes leaning over it.
Uneven stone walls, partly buried in drifts,
Followed it on either side up the hill.
The woods ended and there was the valley,
A white sheet a mile wide, sagging in the middle,
Pinned to the sides of the mountains by scattered trees,
Up to the dark line of spruce and pine.
Then beside the road winding across the valley
Barns and houses emerged.
Clean wood smoke, that made a gray curling shadow on
    the snow,
Rose straight up from kitchen chimneys.
In barnyards cattle stood on the sunny side,
Or crowded by the stable door waiting for milking time.
Some sheep nibbled hay from a fenced-in stack
Which cast a hive-shaped shadow on the snow.
Across a white field a team drew a load of logs.
Steam rose from the panting horses.
A dog ran back and forth in front of them.
The tinkle of their bells came on the crisp air.
The black fence around the white stones stood out on its
    hill,
The stones uneven spots in the smooth covering.
The shadow of the west mountains drew a black line.
It slid slowly across the valley.
The sheep crowded together by the haystack.
The cattle marched in solemn line into the warm barn.
Along the slopes of the eastern mountains
The purple shadow crept up to the last lilac light on the
    highest peak—
Hovering cold, and waiting silence.
Winter night had come to Tinmouth valley.

Chivalry

The Haswell place had once been a good farm.
It began to go down when the sheep business
Had been given over to the West.
The last Haswell to try to run it
Had finally given up and moved to the village.
He rented the place for some years
And then he sold it for what it would bring.
Grover Strong had never paid off the mortgage
And gradually the interest piled up.
That was the only thing that grew there,
Except a little hay in the south meadow.
The rest was going back to forest.

Grover was sitting on the sagging porch
When a city visitor came up the hill.
He greeted Grover and sat down on the step.
He spoke of the view across the valley,
Of the peace of the surrounding woods.
"I suppose it gets pretty well buried in winter,"
He said, feeling he had been showing too much feeling.
Grover allowed it did bank up with snow some.
"I recollect last winter," he said, leaning forward.
"We hed one old heller of a snow storm.
The woman went down t' th' foot th' hill there
T' fetch a couple o' pails o' water from th' spring.
I stood here in th' doorway watchin' 'er.
A gust o' wind 'd come and I couldn't see 'er.
Then it'd quiet down and there she'd be, a-wallerin'."
He sank back in his chair.
"B' gol! They was times I wan't sure she'd make it."

Parsimony

People excused Etta Short's parsimony
On the ground that she had worked so hard
For what little she had.
It was true she had worked hard all her life
But necessary frugality
Had grown into downright miserliness.
She had even held back her affections
So that her children left home as soon as they could,
And left gladly.
She kept on working and saving until she wore out.
Even when she could stay up only part of the day
She wouldn't have any help.
She'd manage to get to the stove and light a fire
Under one griddle, as she always did,
To make herself some tea.
Finally, the daughter stepped in.
She hired a good woman to live with her mother
And she herself came to see her each day.
They said Etta softened up considerably before she died.

When she was in her prime
She told the butcher's boy, one Saturday,
To bring five cents' worth of liver for the cat.
She was having a piece of pork—
The only piece of meat she'd had that week.
When the boy brought her the meat a little later,
She was waiting by the front gate.
"D'je bring me th' liver fer m' cat?"
The boy handed her the small package.
"Well, you kin take it right back.
I don't want it.
The cat jest ketched a bird."

A Horse Trader

Because Stub Hankins was rarely seen
Doing any manual labor
He was looked on by the village as lazy and shiftless.
His place certainly showed no care
And Stub was decidedly neglectful of his appearance.
He was a horse trader by profession,
And in spite of his reputation for laziness
He made a comfortable living at it.
There were times when he was hard up
But most of the time he had plenty for his family,
And not infrequently he was well off.
He was absolutely reliable in his dealings
With anybody but a horse trader.
The village doctors always got their horses from Stub.
He knew what they wanted and saw that they had it.
But his real enjoyment was in trading just to trade.
He knew it was a battle of wits
And that no quarter would be given.
None of the intricacies of high finance
Were ever more devious than the ways of horse traders.

One afternoon Stub drove past the hotel.
He had a mare hitched to the buggy.
"F.H." was standing in front of the hotel
And he called out to Stub:
"Where'd you get that piece of horse-flesh?"
"Traded fer 'er," Stub said.
"How old is she?"
Stub stretched a leg over the dash.
"Wal, the feller said she was fifteen.
He's such a damned liar though,
Like enough she ain't more'n ten."

A Pleasant Rumor

Miss Primer was not a typical old maid.
She was plump and red-cheeked
And she had a nice smile.
She lived alone, to be sure,
But she did not keep a cat nor a canary.
She did have a dog but it was not of the lap variety.
It was a friendly Irish Setter.

Then she had not been without beaus.
She had been popular in her younger days
But somehow men seemed to tire of her.
The impression was that she was too smiling.
Not that she had any real sense of humor.
She really didn't have much of any sense,
And after being in her company for a short time
Her men friends found her quite sickish.
Sometimes they spoke of her as "that sugar bowl."
The time her father was in his last sickness
People would meet her on the street
And ask how he was.
With the usual smile and bubbling manner,
She'd say: "He's worse, thank you."

One day the postmaster handed her the mail.
Looking over his glasses he told her
He'd heard a rumor around town
That she was married.
He hadn't seen her for a few days
And he began to think it must be true.
She smiled and dimpled as usual.
"Oh, no, Mr. Potter, there ain't a word of truth in it."
She looked down at the paper in her hand.
"But thanks for the rumor, Mr. Potter."

Charlie Gets Out of Step

It was back in the Harrison and Morton campaign.
They had a big rally at Bennington,
And every band and drum corps for miles around
Paraded there,
Their brilliant uniforms glittering
In the hot August sun.
After three solid hours of marching
In the heat and dust, they didn't feel so brave
As their uniforms made them appear.
The Drum Corps from our town
Made quite a hit with their snappy rendering
Of the popular campaign airs.
Charlie Williams carried the bass drum.
He had so much of himself in front
That he appeared to carry two drums.
He had refreshed himself frequently,
And as they proceeded along a picket fence
He found it handy to lean against.
He was sliding his elbow along it
When he came to an open gate.
Suddenly missing his support
He and the drum entered the gate precipitately,
Landing in a heap at the foot of three steps.
Frank Bowen, the fifer, ceased playing;
He leaned over the fence and drawled,
"Charlie, ain't yu a leetle mite out o' step?"

A Slow Starter

The day of rain, with clearing that night,
Had resulted in the gathering very early next morning
Of Steve and his two hunting companions.
They'd been waiting for just such a day as was promised.
The rain would have soaked the leaves in the woods
Which had been so dry that every footstep crackled.
The sun had been up long enough in the valley
So by the time they came to the last farm
Up on the east side of the slopes it was warm.
They asked the farmer if they could leave the car
And he told them to run it under a tree by the barn.
He wasn't very talkative and the men were in a hurry
To get those birds they knew were waiting.
They said goodbye and started up the track
That led through the pasture toward the wood.

*   *   *   *   *

The sun was dropping behind the West Mountain
When the three weary hunters came back to the car.
They'd had a grand day, got a few birds,
But found they couldn't walk the way they once could.
They unloaded their guns and stowed them away.
They got out of their hunting coats and boots
And finally settled down in the car,
Looking forward to a restful ride and a real feed
At a place part way home Steve had talked about.
Steve stepped on the starter.
There was a feeble turn of the engine and then just a buzz.
He waited and tried again, with the same result.
He got out and looked under the hood.
They all did the same and each had a suggestion.
The sun had gone and there was a chill in the air.
Abel Stebbens came out of the house with a lantern
And stopped and watched in silence.
"How far to the nearest garage?" one of them asked.
"Down t' the village. 'Bout five miles."

"Could we use your phone?"
"Ain't had one for a year. The woman talked too much."
"How about hitching up a horse and driving to town?"
"Horse's out in the pasture with her shoes off."
They all looked under the hood and poked here and there.
Finally Steve looked at Abel standing there with his lantern.
"Well, have you any suggestion as to what we might do?"
Abel blinked a minute.
"Dunno as I've any suggestions." Another pause.
"But I got a battery."

A Society Note

In the village there was one sure sign
Of fall that was never known to fail.
Eb Stevens would be seen going south
With his wobbly-wheeled lumber wagon,
With sideboards on it, full of apples.
At the back there'd be two battered barrels.
He'd be on his way to Walker's cider mill
That once a year did a thriving business
Squeezing the juice from all kinds of apples.
There was never any effort made to sort the fruit,
Most of which had fallen off the trees voluntarily,
And often showed sure signs of being host to hungry worms.
It might be that, from lying on the ground,
A spot that was quite thoroughly overripe
Would have developed, but all passed through the grinder
At Walker's, tumbling down through the wood chute
From the floor above, where they had been dumped.
Dark brown cloths hung from the line outside
While fresher ones were used to strain the juice
Which ran out from under the presses.
It was caught as it trickled along the soaked planks
In a groove, to be conducted finally
To the deep, dark tub beneath the floor.
There it waited to be drawn off into kegs,
Or jugs, or barrels as the demand required.
It was called "sweet cider" and it really was
In spite of the pervading odor in the mill.
Eb never touched any of this fruit of the tree
Until several weeks or even months had passed.
It happened that his birthday coincided with the date

When considerable potency had developed in his cider,
And it helped to add cheer to the occasion.
One year he had held his usual party
In his rather dilapidated house on the edge of the woods.
When the celebration was over the house
Was much more of a wreck than usual.
The next day found Eb at the store buying window glass,
Points, and putty, and tarred paper to replace one window
Whose frame had been completely demolished.
Eb had been led to speak of the affair to the storekeeper.
Concluding he said: "And I'm givin' notice here an' now
That's the last birthday party I'm givin',
Come what may . . . fer a year, anyhow!"

No Enemies

The G. A. R. Hall was located
Up one flight over Parkinson's Hardware Store.
Faded green window shades at three windows
Proclaimed the fact in gold letters.
Every Thursday evening, from the time roads were open
Until the first of November,
There was a meeting of some kind every two weeks.
As the younger element gradually took over
There were dances and suppers in the winter months.
One spring some of the wives of the Sons of Veterans,
At the suggestion of a few older ones
Who thought there had been too much frivolity,
Announced a series of three lectures on "Life"
The circulars which were handed out after church
Showed a picture of an up and coming young man,
And quoted from various G. A. R. and church groups,
Offering high praise for the young speaker.
He made quite an impression the first night,
But Uncle Ephraim Hubbell, the oldest inhabitant of the village,
Was skeptical, as was his usual custom.
On the last night his curiosity got the better of him.
He sat up near the front so he could hear.
The young speaker was very sure of himself
And his words flowed in fine oratorical style.
After the first few paragraphs Uncle Eph looked around.
There was a cynical half-smile on his wrinkled face.

Suddenly the speaker stopped and moved to the front.
He leaned over toward the audience and said:
"I daresay there is not a person in this audience
Who can honestly say he has not an enemy in the world."
He paused and repeated with a dramatic flourish:
"I ask any man in this audience who has not an enemy to rise."
To the dismay of most of the audience Uncle Eph arose.
Somewhat taken aback the speaker hesitated.
"Well, sir, you look to have had some experience in life."
"Ninety-eight years of it, come next September."
Eph looked around the room and grinned at his friends.
"And you mean to say, sir, that you have not an enemy?"
"That's what I'm standin' up fer."
"Well, er—can you explain how it comes you are so fortunate?"
Uncle Eph squared his shoulders. "Yes, sir, I can and will:
Th' sons of guns are all dead."

Useless Preparation

After her husband died the neighbors worried
About Mrs. Edmunds living in her home alone.
Some of her relatives tried to get her to sell
And move nearer them, but she wouldn't do it.
So she'd gone on living there alone
And as she got used to her loss she made out very well.
She grew older and put on considerable weight
But she still remained pretty.
Looking at her face she didn't seem to have aged much.
Finally the doctor insisted that she must reduce.
At first she rebelled for she did enjoy her food,
But finally she started in on the prescribed diet.
It made her feel strange. She had pains here and there
And she began for the first time to worry about her health.
Then one night after she'd been asleep for a short time
She came suddenly awake and sat up in bed.
She'd never had such a feeling before.
She wasn't really in pain; she just felt strange.
Gradually she came to the conclusion she was going to die.
She wasn't frightened. In fact she found she felt as though
She might be going to embark on an exciting adventure.
Gradually she got back to the present.
She'd always been particular about her appearance

And she decided she couldn't have the undertaker
See her as she was, to say nothing of Saint Peter.
So she got up and turned on the light.
From her bureau she got out a new nightgown she'd had as a gift,
Then the gay dressing gown her niece had sent her.
She put some rouge on her cheeks and powdered her nose.
She even put a little lipstick on.
Then she put out the light and went back to bed.
She awoke from sound sleep to find the room light.
She could see streaks of pink in the east.
She felt hungry, and hastened to the kitchen.
Just then the milkman stopped at the door;
She went out and took the bottle from his hand.
He looked at her in amazement.
"Why, Mis' Edmunds," he said, "you're kinda dressed up
Fer this time o' day ain't ye?"
Shortly he drove off deep in thought.
At the next house where he saw anyone he said:
"Dunno what's come over Mis' Edmunds."
He went on to tell how she was all dressed up
"As though she was goin' somewhere, and then she sez,
'I *was* expectin' to go somewhere, but it wa'n't you
I was expectin' to meet,' sez she."

Metered Service

Every now and then something special happened
Which set the whole village talking.
One year the biggest news to break
Was the buying of an automobile by Ezra Whitcomb.
It was only the fifth car owned in the township
But what made it more surprising was that Ezra,
A conservative in all his opinions and habits,
Should have cut loose with this newfangled buggy . . .
Also that he should have spent six or seven hundred dollars
For something generally considered needless if not useless.
It was a Model T Ford and in the end
Proved to be what Ezra was sure it would be—
A money-saving investment.
It was in running condition when his estate was settled.
Ezra, always known as an "ingenious cuss",
Had rigged up several things

To prevent the need of help on his farm.
Added to that was an inborn dislike of horses.
He had never known how to get along
With the horses he had had to have, but
Of course the machine was never used for pleasure.
Trips down the valley where he did his trading,
And to church on Sunday were about all.
When they put in parking meters down the valley
Ezra vowed he'd never pay the mechanical robbers
And he managed to find free space just beyond them.
One day he found all of his usual free spots full
And as dinner time was drawing near
He gave up and drove into a metered space.
He was so late getting home that day
That his wife met him with an angry laying out.
The whole dinner was either burned or stone cold.
He didn't say a word until he'd had his plate filled.
Then he explained it was those infernal meters.
"Got m' tradin' done and went out.
I found there was still over thirty minutes on the clock.
So I went walkin' round killin' time."
His wife stopped in front of him, dish in hand.
"My lands! What'd you put so much money in it for?"
Ezra took a swallow of coffee.
"Good lord! Think I've gone off m' head?
I didn't put no money in it.
Some feller had left most an hour on the damn thing
When I drove in and hitched there!"

Fence And Offense

It is likely that Alvin Paine
Had never heard of Robert Frost's neighbor,
The one he walked the line with in spring
Mending the wall winter's freezing and thawing
Had made openings in where none were intended.
Certainly if Alvin had ever heard his convictions,
That "Good fences make good neighbors,"
He never showed he took any stock in it.
Either that or else he had no real desire
To be a good neighbor if it required
That he keep his fences mended.
The stone walls had gone before he bought the farm

And in their place former owners
Had strung barbed wire.
Some of the owners had kept it up
And put in new posts at regular intervals.
When Alvin took over, the adjoining farm
Had been abandoned for enough years
That the fences between didn't matter,
And Alvin's cattle soon found places where a rotted post
Had let the wire down.
Now and then the absent owner would write through his lawyer
A legal-sounding letter to Alvin,
And Alvin would drive in a few sapling posts
And collect for most of the new wire
From his neighbor whom he'd never met.
Then a new owner arrived on the scene,
Fixed up the old house and moved his family in.
From the first Alvin could feel trouble coming.
This new man, a George Chapin, began to talk fence.
All spring Alvin was too busy to walk the line.
He promised and then something always came up.
The next Alvin knew he had a stiff letter from a lawyer.
He was threatened with a suit for trespass.
His cows had got into the new neighbor's garden
And had trampled all over the new lawn.
By then a survey had shown that the fence
Was all Alvin's and he was held to be responsible.
It was about then that a large car slowed up
And stopped as Alvin was crossing from the house to the barn.
"Can you tell me where in this neighborhood
My old friend George Chapin lives?" the man asked.
Alvin got his chew placed in his cheek.
"George Chapin? That mis'able whelp?" he asked.
"Never heard of him."
And he hurried across to the barn.

A Little Deaf

Barney Billings had always been known
As something of a ladies' man.
He was small, gentle voiced, and had wavy hair.
He always carried a pocket comb to make sure
That his locks were in perfect order.

For many years he stood at the teller's window
In the bank in the county seat across from the station.
It was said that several of the village females
Had savings accounts at that particular bank
For the thrill of doing business with Mr. Billings.
None of them ever made so bold as to call him "Barney"
He said he never married
Because he found all the ladies so charming
He never could make up his mind.
He just went on loving them all,
And letting them be married to others.
Gradually the years told on Barney Billings.
To outward appearances he was much the same.
There were a few lines showing on his pleasant face
And his hair, still thick and wavy,
Was getting more and more gray.
His worst affliction was his deafness.
He never mentioned it and was very touchy about it.
Suggestions from his nearest friends
That one should speak a little louder to him
Were met with scorn.
Sometimes amazing misunderstandings
Came about because he'd guess at what had been said.
One day the Ladies Aid had a fair
Out on the church lawn.
After it was over Mrs. George Mason,
Who had once been the object of Barney's attentions,
Came into the bank with two or three other "girls".
She was one who still kept a savings account at the bank
And frequently deposited her egg money there.
She handed in a box this time.
"Mr. Billings, this is the Aid money," she said.
As Barney greeted them all, smiling as ever,
And as eager to meet them—though they were all in their sixties;
He hefted the box which had been handed in
And said cheerily,
"The old hens seem to have been doing quite well,
Don't they, this summer?"

An Expert

Alexander Seaton had grown up with logs.
As a child he had played around his father's sawmill
Which was run by the water that came from the brook
Up above the millpond in the pasture.
What the mill needed came down in a wooden flume
Which ran under the road.
Alexander often went with his father
Up the mountain road where timber grew.
Some of it belonged to the Seaton family.
More often Alexander's father would be cutting
On land owned by someone else where he had stumpage rights.
By the time Alexander took over the property
He knew about all there was to know about timber,
From the log to finished lumber.
He was shrewder than the old man, folks found out.
When he bought logs outright he always managed
To pay for fewer feet than there really were.
If he cut over a piece of land
Somehow he managed to get a few logs from the next lot.
His talk was smooth and, anyhow,
It wasn't enough to bring him into court.
He might sell a load of planks with a few short ones
Tucked in where they wouldn't show at first,
Or some off-grade lumber would get mixed in
With what was supposed to be a top grade.
He was always short at the bank so if anyone inquired,
Hoping to get some redress, they'd get little encouragement.
In spite of continual skating upon thin ice
He managed never to fall in.
When, in later years, he got more careful,
And rheumatism kept him from getting around,
He put much of the management into the hands
Of a young chap from out of town who was eager to learn the business
Alexander was careful not to let him know
Too much about his former business methods.
One day two city slickers talked to the young man,
Offering what looked like an attractive deal in pulp wood.
The young man, however, was somewhat suspicious.
Somehow the deal didn't seem quite on the square;
So he decided to counsel with his employer.
He explained the deal and the old man told him

To bring them in and let them talk to him.
"I doubt, young man, if there's any crookedness
Possible in anything to do with lumbering
With which I am not entirely familiar."

Pretty Small Potatoes

The land up at the Southwest Corner
Had always been just right for growing potatoes.
The forest from which it had been cleared
Still surrounded it on three sides.
The soil on the farms still held the richness
Of the ancient forest floor
Built up by years and years of rotting leaves.
One of the best farms for potatoes was Abel Henderson's.
Abel was the third generation on the place
And he had learned to rotate his crops,
And his growing dairy herd
Helped to put back some of the things the ground needed.
But after Abel died his spinster sister took over.
She got rid of Abel's carefully built up dairy
And each year took what she could from her land
With never a thought of returning anything.
She'd always resented Abel's newfangled ways;
Somehow she felt they were an affront to her father.
Henderson's potatoes ceased to be offered for sale.
Finally a young couple rented the farm of Abel's sister.
The young farmer knew his business
And in a few years potatoes from the Henderson farm
Were brought into the county seat as they used to be.
Abel's sister found the income from her share growing
Pleasantly larger and larger as each year passed.
She had always been known as a well-to-do woman
But the church in the valley was her only charity.
She looked on her gifts to it in the nature of insurance.
When the new young minister came to take charge
He was told about Abel's sister, always gloomy and complaining.
As he went up to the farm for his first call
He stopped where the young farmer was digging potatoes.
Long rows of even-sized ones were drying in the sun.
His first greeting to Abel's sister when she came to the door was:
"Good afternoon! What wonderful potatoes in the field down there.

You must be very grateful to our Heavenly Father for such a crop."
Moving a rocker toward him Abel's sister said in a tart voice:
"Things ain't ever so rosy as they seem, Reverend.
Now we haven't got no small ones to feed the hogs."

A Traffic Problem

One of the roads leading out of the valley
Used to wind along a stream to the east.
It followed the curves and even the steep drops
Where the stream rushed madly among the rocks.
Where there were foam-flecked pools
And still water the road, too, leveled out,
Giving a chance for a team coming down
To let up on the breechin' for a little,
Or for one going up to get a deep breath.
Along the ridge there was a view of valley and mountains
Stretching out north and south to enclose the village.
After the stiff climb, along the ridge, were farms.
The highest one, with the best view,
Was the Emerson place, with the fourth generation still on it.
The once big family had scattered by then,
Leaving only Martha and her unambitious husband
On a place which had already begun to run down.
The two places beyond had been abandoned
So the road ended in the Emerson dooryard.
When a summer visitor, fishing along the brook,
Came out at the Emerson place and saw the view
Things began to move so fast for the rather elderly Emersons
That they felt as though they'd been dropped into a whirlpool.
The upshot of it all was that inside of two months
The place was sold for a good price,
And Elmer and Martha Emerson found themselves
Living on a through-road down in the valley.
Along toward fall Elmer was alone with Brayley in the store.
Brayley said how good it must seem
Not to be facing another winter on that lonely hill.
"Well, I tell you, Mr. Brayley," Elmer said,
"It might seem so but this summer's been awful tirin'."
Brayley expressed surprise, thinking they'd have had less work.
"Well, up there t' home, bein' the last house,
When we see or heard a team a'comin' we knew

They was comin' to our place.
Give Marthy a chance t' spruce up a mite.
As 'tis now, when she sees or hears a team a'comin' down the rud,
She like enough thinks, jest as she used to,
They must be a'comin' to see us.
She's about wore out grabbin' up her teeth off th' shelf
And rushin' t' git a clean apron t' cover her dress,
Forty-leven times a day."
He stopped a moment, looking out, and
Then he added: "Nobody stops now."

An Extra Hand

Strangers coming to the valley
Were sure to want to know what the large white spot was
Which showed half way up the peak to the north.
Some of the older ones remembered when the spot
Had been so small it hardly showed at all.
It was the waste dump of the old Fulsom Quarry
Which was cut straight into the side of the mountain.
The entrance was rather narrow.
The main quarry opened to the view like a great hall
With its walls rising a hundred feet or more.
The floor was almost level and the years
Had given time for bushes and small trees
To find dirt enough to get a roothold.
In clefts high up a few birches perched
And there was green moss against the white.
The once busy dump in front had gathered soil enough
To let grass grow making a smooth lawn
Kept clipped by sheep and cattle which wandered up
From the pasture down below.
Standing there the valley lay open, with the mountains
Showing where the river cut through to the west.
On a clear day, twenty miles south where another peak
Seemed to close the valley,
The shaft of the battle monument showed
Like a tall white spire against the green.
A big order from a New York contractor,
Who wanted just the kind of marble the Fulsom Quarry
Had furnished years before,
Had suddenly brought the mountain to life.

James Bundy, who always said he'd been raised on marble,
Advertised for a hundred men to go to work at once.
There had been slack times and more than two hundred
Had thronged into the yard around the small office.
Toward mid-afternoon the hundred had been picked.
James was leaning back in his chair, relaxed,
When a tall lank man opened the door.
His face fell when he heard the men had all been hired.
Finally he spoke of his large family and sickness.
"I need the work, Mr. Bundy, and need it bad."
James smoked and looked out of the window.
The man turned and then came back and said, half smiling,
"I wish you'd take me on. Why, say,
I wouldn't do enough work to make a mite of difference."
James Bundy let his chair down and reached for his book:
"What'd you say your name was?" he asked
With a twinkle in his eye.

Unchanged

After Steve Elder's wife died,
Having worn herself out over the washtub,
Folks wondered what Steve would do.
His chief occupation for years had been
Gathering washes for his wife to do
And taking them back when the ironing had been done.
He'd gradually given up working around his small place
When he found the laundry business paid.
His berry bushes had borne little for several years
And were a tangle of brush and weeds,
Even his small garden got less and less attention.
The last cow he'd had wasn't half fed
And folks said some of the time
Steve's wife did the milking while Steve
Sat by the fire and complained about his health.
He generally managed to get down to the store
And do considerable loafing, usually after the effort
Of delivering a washing somewhere with his wheelbarrow.
He used some of the money from the laundry business
To buy patent medicines like Peruna,
Which was a cheap grade of whiskey
With a few other things added for conscience sake.

Then all at once Steve found himself alone
With his visible means of support having the first rest
She'd had since the year after she married Steve.
Then a kind Providence again stepped in.
Steve sold his fifteen acres with its fine view
To a man from Boston who built on top of the hill.
Somehow Steve spruced up enough to impress the buyer
And he was left in his house and given a job as gardener.
Folks in the village, realizing how hard
His wife had worked all the years to support him,
Were amazed and provoked when Steve really did manage
To get a fairly good garden the first year.
It wasn't long before he was telling his employer
How he'd have to give up doing this or that,
Always bemoaning how he used to be able to do
What sounded like two men's work any day.
By the second year the newcomer had to hire more help
And in the end Steve really became a pensioner.
The newcomer was speaking of Steve in the store one day.
"Well, I guess poor Steve isn't the man he used to be," he said.
"No, I guess mebbe he isn't," Brayley said.
One of the sitters added tartly:
"No, he ain't, and he never was, by judast!"

Day Of Rest

Early and late, day in and day out,
Six days a week, Joshua Champon was sure to be working.
He had a place just outside the village,
Only a matter of some forty acres in all,
And part of that was a small sugar bush.
He never kept more than three or four cows
And his one horse easily took care
Of the things manpower couldn't handle.
Of course he had a pig and some chickens.
Not only was Joshua always at work—
He always was in a hurry about whatever he did.
He'd hoe his potatoes as though he were a warrior
Attacking the enemy with all he had in him.
It was the same way when he swung a scythe or an ax.
The only time when he was known to sit for any length of time
Was when he went to Mid-week Prayer Meeting

And on Sunday mornings when he sat in his pew at church.
Even on the Sabbath, when only the most necessary things were done,
He did those few things as though he were driven.
Keeping the Sabbath was a matter of real discipline.
The cooking had been done the day before.
The cattle were milked, fed and watered, or let out to pasture;
The other livestock was attended to as simply as possible.
What there was of the Sabbath not taken up
With services and Sunday school,
Was spent in reading the Bible or napping.
On that one day only, inside or outside of the Champon house,
There was quiet and silence, and almost complete immobility.
One such morning Joshua came into the kitchen from the barn.
When he explained why he was a little later than usual
His wife looked at him in horror.
It took some talk to convince him
That it wasn't Saturday but the Sabbath—the Day of Rest.
Without a thought of breakfast, set on the table,
Joshua rushed out toward the barn.
This time he did really run—and to beat the Devil.
He had spent his usual half hour cleaning out the cow-stable.
In less than half that time, driven by a guilty conscience,
He shoveled everything back.
The Champon family arrived at the Meeting House
Only a few minutes later than usual;
Which was generally half an hour early.

Road Conditions

What had started as a fine spring morning
Had turned to dark cloud threats by afternoon;
By four o'clock it was raining steadily.
As Henry Barstow, who was headed for a schoolhouse meeting
In a town he'd never heard of until that morning,
Drove along the muddy, lonesome road,
He wondered why he'd volunteered to take the place
Of the other young theological student who couldn't go.
Now and then he passed a farmhouse dimly lighted,
And he once saw a lantern moving from barn to barn.
He began to wonder whether he had the right road.
The directions to East Cambridge had sounded clear enough,
But in the wet darkness he might miss a turn.

He tried to go over what he was going to say.
What he'd hurriedly outlined as a brief sermon
Seemed about as uncertain in his mind as the road ahead.
Finally he decided to stop at the next house near the road
And make sure of his directions.
Around a turn he came on a lighted house.
Holding his coat tight around his neck
He ran for the porch under the dripping maples.
After a second hard knock an elderly woman
Opened the door cautiously, letting a V of light
Out into the wet darkness of the surrounding trees.
Learning what the caller wanted she called her husband.
He came from the kitchen, a red checked napkin
Tucked into his collar.
"To get t' East Cambridge?" He rubbed his chin.
"Ain't been there in years. No call t' go.
Let's see, East Cambridge. Bad night t' be travelin'.
East Cambridge. Well, go down this rud some two miles.
Turn off to th' right by the schoolhouse.
Go along about a half mile and turn right again.
Then, let' see. Take th' next left . . . er no,
That goes over t' Skunk Holler. Take th' second left.
Now hold on. You want t' go t' East Cambridge?
Well, turn off by th' schoolhouse as I said and then
Turn . . ." He rubbed his chin again and discovered
The napkin. He took it out and used it to flag directions.
"Come t' think of it, you go straight ahead
After turnin' at the schoolhouse I told yu 'bout.
Yessir. That's right, young feller. Straight ahead."
Still somewhat uncertain Henry Barstow thanked him.
As he started down the steps the old man called:
"That's right. Straight ahead, as I said.
If you don't find yerself in East Cambridge
I'll be allfired surprised."

Non-Central Heating

The woodshed was almost as important
In the houses in any village
As the kitchen whose generous stove it fed.
When a few of the more well-to-do or progressive families
Had coal-burning stoves set up

They still used wood for the kitchen.
Most of the farmhouses stuck to wood.
There wasn't much use in spending hard cash for coal
When there was plenty of good fuel on the woodlot.
And, after all, with a bright wood fire
Crackling in the big kitchen range,
Throwing flickering shadows on the ceiling,
There wasn't any other spot offering so much real comfort.
In one such kitchen there was a row of wooden chairs
Back of the stove with arms worn smooth by three generations
Of men who had sat there when they came in from the barn.
In the sitting room there was a coal-burner
Of the self-feeding kind with mica windows in the doors
So that the sight of the fire might help with the warmth.
Miss Elkins, the last of the well-to-do Elkins family,
Had coal stoves in all downstairs rooms, even the hall,
And a small one in her bedroom.
The man-of-all-work usually looked after them.
He was getting well along in years
And was too lame to tackle a pipe cleaning job
Which failure to draw evidently demanded.
Miss Elkins was very pious and she was quite shocked
When she found it was Cabe Morse he'd got to do the job.
Cabe was known to have a large cussing vocabulary.
"Mr. Morse," Miss Elkins said when he came in,
"I want it fully understood that I will not allow
The name of the Lord to be taken in vain in my house."
Cabe expressed surprise that she'd think of such a thing.
Mounting a box he started pulling down the pipe.
It stuck and he twisted and pulled and yanked;
Finally it gave way all at once.
Cabe and the soot-laden pipe fell together.
Miss Elkins stood off with her hand over her mouth
As though she expected a blow on the face.
Cabe arose slowly and looked around.
He bowed toward Miss Elkins and said in a solemn voice:
"Let us pray."

The Professor Has Callers

When the Professor first saw the farm
He was so delighted with the view
That he forgot many practical matters,
While his wife was prowling around inside
Overcome by the accumulation of decay
Especially evident in the upstairs rooms.
The Professor was forever turning to the front windows
High enough to show the stretch of hills and valleys
With uneven lines of mountains as a background.
He had already removed the weatherbeaten barn
Which cut off much of the view from the porch.
He even then felt peace sinking into his soul
As he sat on the stone terrace he'd built
To replace the sagging porch across the front.
The tumbled stone walls he pictured
As surrounding the garden to the east of the house.
He'd found somewhere stored deep in his mind
A yearning to build a stone wall.
As they drove back to the village
The appalling defects which his wife saw,
Already pressing down on her as a good housekeeper,
And the burden of the cost of repairing the place,
Failed to daunt the determination of the Professor,
And before nightfall he owned the view.
One summer, several years later, the Professor
Was busy getting his garden going behind the stone wall
His own hands had built during summer vacations.
He was enjoying the freedom of old work-stained clothes.
When a car stopped on the road he didn't look up.
A harsh voice broke the quiet of his task.
"Hey there!" He paid no attention to the call.
"Hey there, I say!" came in a more disrespectful tone.
The third call made the Professor turn in anger.
Slowly he walked toward the car.
Before the insolent visitors could ask a question
The Professor gazed at them steadily and repeated
In Latin several impressive lines from Pliny
Which seemed to apply to the case in hand.
Then he turned and went back to his gardening.
Still with their mouths open the visitors drove away.

Profanity

Mrs. Appleby was having a tea party.
The sun shone in on her plants
Which filled the south-facing bay window
And there was a not-too-ardent fire
Simmering in the Franklin grate at the other end of the room.
As always her white curtains were crisp and immaculate,
Looking like the dresses of little girls
Starched and ruffled for the exercises on the last day of school.
The canary chirped from his cage
As he tipped his head and hopped on and off his perch
Somewhat excited by the extra voices.
Mrs. Appleby's best china was on the tea tray
And some of her famous finger biscuits.
Her guests, four of them, were all leaning forward
To catch what Miss Gramby was saying.
Miss Gramby was so gentle and mild in voice and manner
That on the infrequent occasions when she spoke
Everyone stopped to listen.
They had to pay close attention to hear.
When she spoke she exercised all of her face;
Twisting her rather large mouth
To get the full value of every word as though she were singing.
The first topic for the conversation in the group
Had been the recent elopement of a school teacher,
With one of the wilder young men of the village,
Leaving the school without an instructor.
Several had expressed their opinions
When Miss Gramby began to twist and turn,
Always a signal that she was about to speak.
Her first remark, made in her usual mild voice
And slow manner of speaking, had electrified them all.
"If I knew how, I'd really swear," she said,
Telling of her feelings about the elopement.
To the amazement of all, she went on at some length
Venting her wrath not on the man but on the girl.
Her cheeks got pink and then red as she talked.
Finally her voice broke and she stopped talking.
She grabbed her small cloth handbag and half standing
She slung it across the room.
"There," she said in an unusually strong voice,
"That's a swear."

On A Rainy Day

It had been raining during the night
And after breakfast it looked like more downfall.
When Ephraim announced that he might drive down the valley
Amanda, his wife, suggested things to be done at home.
She wasn't in sympathy with some of her husband's trips.
They always involved trading horses.
It often happened that a horse she especially liked
Would be replaced by a new one
Just to satisfy his mania for trading.
Ephraim drove out of the yard and turned down the valley.
Cabe Elder was out in front of his house
And he beckoned to Eph to turn in.
It seemed he had a horse, sound and true,
But he wanted something for the road.
Eph didn't show any interest at first.
He did get out and look Cabe's horse over.
"Mandy, she's taken a shine t' this mare here," he said.
A half hour later he drove down the valley
Behind Cabe's horse with a ten dollar bill in his wallet.
Down at the Falls a friend told him
There was a fellow with some horses at the horse sheds;
He'd come from over New Hampshire way.
Eph proved himself a match for these foreign traders
And finally drove toward home with a likely mare
And several crisp bills added to his roll.
As he neared the village he saw Cabe Elder
Going from the house to the barn.
He waved to Cabe and Cabe set down his pails and beckoned.
He'd watched Eph come across the flats.
"See you traded again," he said.
"Kinda like the action of this one as I see you
Comin' up across the flats."
He was a mite disappointed in the one he'd got that morning.
"She wasn't quite the roader I thought she was," he said.
Eph gradually got interested and Cabe got in
And drove down the road a piece.
A half hour later Eph drove into his own yard.
He'd just gotten the horse unhitched when Amanda came into the barn.
The horse turned and went straight to the watering trough
And then came back to its old stall.

Amanda looked at Eph, her hands on her hips.
"Well," she said, "you can't tell me the old story
That you been tradin' all day.
Got the same horse you drove out with,
Just as I thought when I see you go past the kitchen."
Eph smiled a little and reached into his pocket.
"Yes, Mandy," he said, "it's the same old hoss,
But this here roll—that's all new, by judast!"

A Wartime Auction

The front yard of the old Hammond farmhouse
Was filled with people the day George had his auction.
He was selling off everything except what was needed
For him and Alice to set up housekeeping again
In the small house they'd bought in the village.
The new owner of the farm, which had been in the Hammond family
For four generations,
Had bought the livestock and machinery.
Now they were selling the household things they didn't need,
And the machinery the new owner didn't want.
Deciding to sell had been hard for George and his wife,
But it seemed the only thing to do . . now that there'd be
No one to inherit the farm.
The auctioneer had moved the steps away from the porch
And the crowd stood around under the maples.
On the outer rim neighbors exchanged family news.
Here and there a soldier or a sailor, home on leave,
Was enjoying for a moment the return to familiar life.
But some of the Hammond's neighbors couldn't share
The holiday mood of the crowd.
Miss Henshaw sat unsmiling at the jokes of the auctioneer.
She knew too much about the tragedy of the auction—
Her memory recalled too vividly the days of hope
And happiness when Dave was growing into a fine
Stalwart boy of whom the whole village was fond.
Finally she got up from her seat and wandered around back.
There were the larger pieces, like bedroom sets and tables,
Leaning against the side of the house—
All of the things she'd known for years
Now looking like outcasts on the grass.

It was getting near chore time when Miss Henshaw
Got into the car of a neighbor who offered her a lift.
"Well," she said looking back at the house,
"There'll never be another Hammond living there.
Sometimes it seems as though I can't bear to think of it."
The neighbor looked the other way. "Tough," he said.
The crowd had all gone when the sun dropped behind the mountain.
George was waiting in the pick-up truck,
Piled high with a few last things.
His wife went into the empty parlor where the shadows were gathering.
She walked to the window and took down the service flag
With its one gold star.

Wartime Memorial Day, 1944

Perhaps it is only natural that his stone
Should mean much more to us this year.
Of course we knew he was only seventeen when he went;
And we knew that here, in the burying ground, there had never
Been anything but his stone.
It read "Died at Yorktown" and we knew it was of pestilence
And not in battle that he died.
We seem to remember Grandfather telling of his fruitless
Search for the body;
And his return with nothing to tell—but that.
Now we fall to wondering about the day the boy left.
What did his mother, our grandmother, do when the train had gone?
There are letters he wrote.
They tell of the trip to New York and about Washington,
And the camp outside the city, but hardly a hint of war,
Except some tale of "Johnny Reb", usually funny.
Some news too about the other town boys,
And much about the food sent from home.
Then a letter that told of rumors of moving:
And after that nothing more—then or ever.
And now another generation is writing about camps,
And about home-sent cookies,
But hardly a word about war,
Except hints and rumors.
We wonder how Grandmother took his going

Those first few days when habit made her hear his voice
As she tidied up his room against his coming home . . .
His coming home . . .
She'd borne six children but he was her first born.
From what we know of her she kept right on,
Busy with the ordinary things of normal life.
If we could only see one letter that she wrote to him,
Then we could know what gave her strength.

                    . . . . . .

And then the day the message came;
And the later day when Grandfather set out on his fruitless
    search,
Which of the younger sons took him to the train,
And what was said?
How was it between the father and those sons?
What did they talk about
Waiting with their mother during those dragging days?
And how did Grandfather tell them his search had failed,
And how did each one take it?
Could they then see any glory in cold history
Written in blood so warm?
If we now knew how it was with them,
Out of that past, we might build a bulwark
To shield us in these days.